SCI-FI TECH

WHAT WOULD IT TAKE TO MAKE A
FLYING CAR?

BY MEGAN RAY DURKIN

CAPSTONE PRESS
a capstone imprint

Capstone Captivate is published by Capstone Press, an imprint of Capstone.
1710 Roe Crest Drive
North Mankato, Minnesota 56003
www.capstonepub.com

Library of Congress Cataloging-in-Publication Data is available on the Library of Congress website.
ISBN: 978-1-5435-9116-3 (library hardcover)
ISBN: 978-1-4966-6596-6 (paperback)
ISBN: 978-1-5435-9124-8 (eBook PDF)

Summary: Describes how the science-fiction concept of flying cars could be made in real life, including the scientific concepts involved, the progress that scientists have made, and what the future could hold.

Image Credits
Getty Images: Imagno/Hulton Archive, 7; iStockphoto: Chesky_W, 8–9, 13; Newscom: Imagine China, 17, mavrixonline.com/Terrafugia, 15, 28–29, PAL-V/Cover Images, 18, Wang Gang/SIPA ASIA/Pacific Press, 16; Shutterstock Images: Antonello Marangi, 19, Costazzurra, 4, 24–25, 27, d13, 21, Marco Wong, cover (background), metamorworks, 22, Pavel Chagochkin, cover (car), Skycolors, 23, u3d, 10
Design Elements: Shutterstock Images

Editorial Credits
Editor: Arnold Ringstad; Designer: Laura Graphenteen

Printed in the United States of America.
PA99

TABLE OF CONTENTS

WORDS IN BOLD ARE IN THE GLOSSARY.

Flying cars could change the way we think about transportation.

CHAPTER ONE

CARS IN THE SKY

The sound of honking horns fills the air. Cars all around are creeping slowly along the road. It's another traffic jam in the city. High above, an airplane soars freely through the sky. What if cars could do the same thing? Some people think flying cars are the future of transportation. Traffic jams could become a thing of the past.

People have dreamed about flying cars for years. But challenges keep getting in the way. Building these vehicles is hard. It costs a lot of money. And keeping people safe while using them is tricky. Designers today are working through these challenges. New flying cars are being tested. Someday you may be able to zoom above cities in your own flying car!

CHAPTER TWO

WHAT IS A FLYING CAR?

People have dreamed of flying like birds for a long time. Inventors have been drawing flying machines for hundreds of years. In the early 1900s, the dream became a reality. People invented airplanes.

Cars became common around the same time. People could drive themselves from place to place. What if the best parts of cars and airplanes could be combined? A car could turn into a flying machine.

FLYING CAR HISTORY

The magazine *Popular Science* has stories about the latest inventions. It has been covering flying cars since the 1920s. One model from 1926 had fold-up wings. Another from 1952 had wings that came off. Some of these models look silly today. But they were steps along the way to today's flying cars.

People have long thought
of mixing cars and planes.

What would a flying car do? It would be able
to both fly and drive. This would give drivers
more freedom.

Flying cars could soar over traffic on the ground.

Imagine a person is visiting a friend in another state. The person flies to the other state. The traveler lands at an airport. Finally he drives on the road from the airport to his friend's house. A flying car would make this possible.

Rotors could lift flying cars into the air.

CHAPTER THREE

HOW WOULD A FLYING CAR WORK?

A flying car has to be able to drive and fly. Some parts are used for both these jobs. The vehicle needs a body to protect the people inside. The flying car needs wheels and tires for driving. It also needs a way to steer.

Even more parts are needed for flying. There are two major ways for flying cars to travel through the air. The first way uses wings and a **propeller**. The propeller pushes the car forward. The wings create **lift**. The second way to fly uses **rotors**. Rotors push air downward. This pushes the car into the air. This is the way a helicopter flies.

Cars and planes both use engines. Engines burn **fuel** to create motion. In a car this turns the wheels. In a plane this spins the propeller. Often flying cars have separate engines. One is for flying. Other motors power the wheels.

A flying car also needs a way to help the driver know where to go. Traveling on roads is fairly easy. You just need to know which turns to take. Flying is harder. You can fly almost anywhere. You can soar high into the sky or fly near the ground. The **Global Positioning System** (GPS) can help people get to where they want to go.

What about emergencies? If a car suddenly stops working, it simply stops moving. But if a plane stops working, it falls out of the sky. Flying cars need gear such as parachutes so they can fall safely.

PARTS OF A FLYING CAR

propeller

tire

foldable wings

tail

CHAPTER FOUR

CURRENT TECH

Many companies are working on flying cars. None of their vehicles are widely available yet. But designers continue to make them better.

One example comes from a company called Terrafugia. It calls its flying car the Transition. In flying mode it looks like a small airplane. The Transition has wide wings. A propeller in the back pushes it through the air. In driving mode the wings fold up. Electric motors power the four wheels.

BUYING A FLYING CAR

Flying cars will be very expensive. In 2018, Terrafugia said it would begin selling the Transition soon. The cost would be around $400,000.

The Transition's wings lift upward and fold over in driving mode.

The AeroMobil has received a lot of attention from flying car fans.

Another flying car is the AeroMobil. It works like the Transition. A propeller pushes it along in the air. It uses electric motors for driving. But AeroMobil's wings fold backward instead of up. The propeller folds away when driving too. AeroMobil flies twice as fast as the Transition. Its engine is much more powerful.

The AeroMobil has a wide wingspan.

The PAL-V flies more like a helicopter than an airplane.

The PAL-V works differently than the Transition and the AeroMobil. The PAL-V looks like a helicopter. This flying car has no wings. It has rotors instead. The rotors carry the PAL-V into the air. A propeller in the back pushes the flying car forward through the air.

The Pop.Up Next is a totally different idea. It has no wings or rotors. It cannot fly on its own. For short trips, the **self-driving** car drives the user around. For longer trips, the car sends a message to a **drone**. The drone comes and picks up the car. The drone has four rotors. It looks like a huge version of a toy drone. It carries the car to where the user wants to go. Then it flies away. When it's time for another long trip, another drone comes.

The Pop.Up Next separates its flying part from its driving part.

CHAPTER FIVE

WHAT TECH IS NEEDED?

Most current flying cars run on fuels that create **pollution**. An engine burns the fuel. The engine makes the propellers or rotors spin.

Pollution harms the environment. People want to use electricity for flying cars. This will make them better for the environment. It also creates new challenges. Current **batteries** that would store enough energy to power the vehicle are heavy. This extra weight makes it harder for the vehicle to fly. Battery technology must improve.

FUN FACT

One company has a new idea to power flying cars. It wants to use very long cords from the ground. Small batteries would give cars the power to land safely if the cords broke.

Many cars now use electricity for power. Flying cars might someday do the same.

Self-driving technology is getting better quickly. New versions of it could be used in flying cars.

Flying is a lot harder than driving. Drivers speed up or slow down. They turn left or right. Pilots must do more. They have to look above and below. They have to take off and land. A crash could be deadly.

Some planes today have self-flying systems. They can handle some parts of a flight. Modern airliners can land themselves.

One way to solve this is to let computers steer flying cars instead. They would use **sensors** to avoid other vehicles in the air. The user would just sit back and enjoy the ride. Experts are working on these self-flying systems. The computers and sensors will need to improve. People's lives will depend on them.

A system called autopilot helps pilots fly airplanes. Flying cars could use similar systems.

Flying cars create new dangers. What if an engine fails in the middle of a city? The flying car could fall out of the sky. This would be dangerous for the people in the flying vehicle and those below. Companies must find ways to make flying cars safe.

Flying cars will pass over homes and other buildings. This makes safety very important.

Parachutes can slow a flying car's fall. Backup engines can keep it flying if one engine fails. Experts are searching for other ways to reduce dangers.

CHAPTER SIX

WHAT COULD THE FUTURE LOOK LIKE?

Flying cars could change the future of transportation. Imagine you are traveling to your grandma's house. You know it usually takes three hours to drive there. But now you have a flying car. You back out of the garage. A small airport is a few minutes away. It is just for flying cars. You drive there.

At the airport, the wings fold out. The engine powers the propeller instead of the wheels. You roll down the runway. Once you are fast enough, you gently lift into the air. The computer steers you to your grandma's city. When you arrive, the computer lands the flying car safely at another airport. Then you drive the last few minutes to your grandma's house. The whole trip took just an hour.

Long trips could become much quicker with flying cars.

Flying cars could be found in garages all over the world someday.

Flying cars have been science fiction for a long time. But soon they may become reality. Better batteries, smarter computers, and good safety gear will be needed. The vehicles will also need to get cheaper. If those things happen, we may see flying cars zooming through cities soon. Would you take a ride in a flying car? What's the first place you would go?

GLOSSARY

battery (BAT-uh-ree)—a device that stores energy in the form of electricity

drone (DROHN)—a flying machine that does not have a pilot and is controlled from the ground

fuel (FYOOL)—a material burned to give off energy

Global Positioning System (GLOW-bull puh-ZI-shuhn-ing SIS-tum)—an electronic tool that receives signals from satellites in the sky to find the location of objects on Earth

lift (LIFT)—a force that pushes objects upward

pollution (poh-LOO-shun)—materials that harm the air, water, and land and make them dirty

propeller (pro-PELL-ur)—a device that spins to push a vehicle forward

rotor (ROH-tur)—a device that spins to push a vehicle upward

self-driving (self DRY-ving)—able to move without a person's control

sensor (SEN-sur)—a device that can see, hear, or detect its surroundings

READ MORE

Bethea, Nikole Brooks. *High-Tech Highways and Super Skyways: The Next 100 Years of Transportation*. North Mankato, MN: Capstone Press, 2017.

Chandler, Matt. *The Tech Behind Self-Driving Cars*. North Mankato, MN: Capstone Press, 2020.

Lanier, Wendy Hinote. *Flying Cars*. Lake Elmo, MN: Focus Readers, 2019.

INTERNET SITES

DK Find Out: Flying Car Facts
https://www.dkfindout.com/us/transportation/history-cars/flying-car/

Smithsonian: The Invention of the Flying Car
https://www.smithsonianchannel.com/videos/the-invention-of-the-flying-car/20504

Wonderopolis: What Will You Drive When You Grow Up?
https://www.wonderopolis.org/wonder/what-will-you-drive-when-you-grow-up

INDEX